A Gift For

....

From

....

The Little Book of
BEDTIME
BLESSINGS

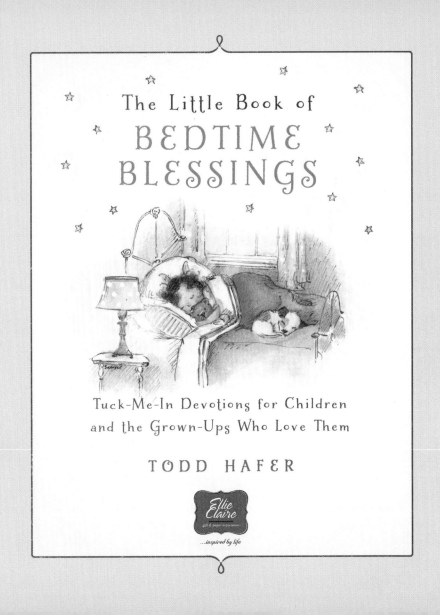

Tuck-Me-In Devotions for Children
and the Grown-Ups Who Love Them

TODD HAFER

Ellie
Claire
gift & paper expressions

...inspired by life

Ellie Claire™ Gift & Paper Corp.
Brentwood, TN 37027
EllieClaire.com

The Little Book of Bedtime Blessings
Tuck-Me-In Devotions for Children and the Grown-Ups Who Love Them

© 2013 by Todd Hafer

ISBN 978-1-60936-753-4

Cover illustration by Julie Sawyer Phillips
Cover and interior design by Thinkpen Design | ThinkpenDesign.com

Ellie Claire Gift & Paper Corp. is an imprint of Worthy Publishing.

Printed in China

To Jody, T.J., Jami Jo, Taylor,
Olivia, and Kaycee.
To even imagine
a better family
would be preposterous.

Praise be to the God and Father
of our Lord Jesus Christ, who has
blessed us in the heavenly realms with
every spiritual blessing in Christ.

EPHESIANS 1:3

Contents

Introduction

I Need a Time Machine (Cheap)

I need a time machine. It doesn't have to be a top-of-the line model. An off-brand will be fine. Slightly used. Scratched and/or dented. I'll make do.

It doesn't even need to be that powerful.

Sure, I would love to get writing tips from Shakespeare, run sprint intervals with Jesse Owens, and beg Abe Lincoln for leadership lessons. And, if only I could go back two thousand years! I am nowhere near good enough to be a disciple of Jesus. But maybe Sandal Repair Guy? I would settle for that.

But such a machine would be out of my price range. And I would be too tech-challenged to operate it. So give me a contraption

that will nudge me back just a few years. To an age when I shared bedtime stories with my four kids. Some from favorite books, some from the dusty and disorganized garage that is my mind.

Many of these stories ended with me stumbling my way through a blessing for the kid in question. I'm not an officially licensed blessing-giver, but those moments meant something. To the grown-up as much as child, I think. We were brushing against something sacred.

Here in 2013, my kids' bedtime-story days are done. How can I compete with Skype, the iPhone, the iPad, and the iDon't-Even-Know-What-That-Device-Is!

But sometimes when I pass my teenagers' rooms, where there is almost always furious texting, tweeting, and tumblr-ing in progress, I whisper a quiet blessing. And I pray, "Lord, I hope that one took."

The way I see it, kids outgrow a lot of things. But does anyone ever outgrow being blessed?

—Todd Hafer

A Bit About the Blessings...

A variety of short blessings end each of this book's readings. Some are written to be spoken to the child, pronounced over him or her, like a pastor blesses a congregation. Occasionally, you'll see a fill-in-the-blank space, where you can insert a child's name, personalizing the blessing.

Other blessings are penned in the first person, so that grown-up and child can read them together.

Some of the blessings are traditional and presented in their original form. In many cases, I have updated the language—while striving to maintain the spirit of the original. You'll see blessings from around the world, and from some of my favorite writers.

Others are originals—blessings I have used with the kids in my life.

As you'll see, many of the blessings are inspired by the Bible, with Scripture references provided.

Truly, it was a blessing to write this book. I pray that it will be a blessing to share it with the child or children you love.

Together Is Better

You could learn a lot from a penguin. Really.

Emperor penguins live in a place called Antarctica, near the bottom of the world. It's the coldest place on earth. So these penguins know the importance of sticking together. They huddle together by the thousands, sharing warmth that allows them to survive the ice-cold weather. (Did you know it gets so cold in Antarctica that hard steel can snap like a potato chip?)

Emperor penguins take turns standing guard on the outside of their giant huddle, on the lookout for danger, or food. After a while, these "guard penguins" get to move inside the huddle so they can get warm.

The baby penguins stand on their moms' and dads' feet, so that they don't have to stand on ice or snow.

Here's what we can learn from penguins: No matter where we live—Antarctica, Africa, Arizona, or Alabama—it's a good idea to stick together. That's why God gives us family and friends. These people teach us, protect us, and, most of all, love us.

And, of course, if it gets cold, they can help us get warm too. Just like penguins.

Be kind to one another, tenderhearted, forgiving one another, as God in Christ forgave you.

EPHESIANS 4:32 ESV

Dear God, may You always surround this precious child with people whose hearts are full of love. May their love reflect Your love, the greatest love of all! Amen.

A Baby Named Jesus

Jesus was a grown-up man when He traveled the countryside more than two thousand years ago, healing people and teaching them how to live a good life.

But He first came to earth as a tiny infant, just as you did. When an infant is born, he or she weighs only about seven pounds—about as much as a house cat. Newborns are completely helpless. They need grown-ups for protection and food.

Jesus chose to come to earth as a tiny baby so that He could grow up and experience what it's like to be a person—a person just like *you*.

Jesus had to learn to walk and talk, just like you. He fell down and got hurt sometimes. He was probably bullied by some mean kids. He had bad dreams that made Him wake up, crying and calling out for Mom and Dad.

So when you pray to Jesus, you're talking to someone who knows what it's like to be *you*. He knows how you feel. He understands you. And, most important, Jesus loves you! He always will, no matter what age you are!

*The child Jesus grew. He became strong
and wise, and God blessed him.*

LUKE 2:40 CEV

Father God,
You could have sent Your Son Jesus to earth
as a giant super-hero, but You sent Him as a
tiny baby instead. Jesus grew up, just as this
little one is growing up. Jesus understands what
it's like to be a kid. May Your love be upon
_____ [child's name] through every
age of childhood, and for every age after that!

Faith Is Like a Nightlight

Do you sleep with a nightlight in your room? (Or did you when you were a bit younger?)

Nightlights are a good thing. They aren't so bright that they keep you from falling asleep, but they are bright enough to help you see where you are going if you wake up in the middle of the night and need to get a drink or use the bathroom. And, let's just say it: A nightlight can help your room be less scary. A nightlight is like a little ray of hope. It's a promise that morning is coming. It won't be dark for too long.

A nightlight is also a message to a young boy or girl: "The people in your house care a whole lot about you. That's why we put this light here for you."

Did you know that faith in God is kind of like a nightlight? Faith is the light that gives you hope. By believing in God and talking to Him, you can get through scary things. But here's how faith and nightlights are a little different: Faith is like a light *inside you*, rather than outside of you. Faith reminds you that God loves you very, very much. You are never alone. Wherever you go, God's light and God's love are with you always.

Think how much the Father loves us. He loves us so much that he lets us be called his children, as we truly are.

1 John 3:1 CEV

Dear God, may You be this child's light always. May Your light give comfort. May Your words and the example of Jesus show this little one how to live a good and happy life. May this precious child always feel the warmth of Your light, glowing and shining inside.

Gifts with No Gift Wrap

Think of the best present you ever got. Maybe it was a birthday present. Maybe it was a Christmas gift, wrapped up under a big tree.

But did you know that not ALL gifts are wrapped up and delivered? God gives us *all* kinds of gifts every day. When your mom or dad or Sunday school teacher says, "Good job!"—that's a gift. So is a hug from Grandma or a high-five from your best friend. God fills the world with wonderful gifts for us. And we don't have to wait for special occasions to get them.

If we open our hearts—and our eyes—we can be filled up every day with gifts that remind us that God is on our side and that His heart is full of love for us!

And did you know that the Bible says that children like you are a gift too? It's true! You are a gift to all the people who love you!

Children are a gift from God; they are his reward.

PSALM 127:3 TLB

Lord, we offer You thanks and praise.
For the gift of all our days.
For all Your gifts, of every kind.
We offer praise, with heart and mind.
Be with me, Lord, and guide my ways.
Through all my nights, through all my days.

INSPIRED BY ST. FRANCIS OF ASSISI

It's Good to Monkey Around!

It's not easy being a snow monkey. Japan's snow monkeys have to work very hard just to stay alive. They spend a lot of their time climbing high, cold mountains, always looking for food. However, a snow monkey's life is not all work and no play.

Snow monkeys take breaks. They rest. They chill out. They even monkey around a little! If they didn't refresh like this, they would be tired all of the time.

Now, you don't have to climb high snowy mountains to search for food. But your body, mind, and soul all need rest sometimes. So eat a healthful snack when you are hungry. A banana, perhaps?

Get plenty of sleep. And if your world gets too loud and busy, find a quiet place. Rest easy, little monkey.

Your heavenly Father already knows all your needs.
Seek the Kingdom of God above all else,
and live righteously, and he will give you everything
you need. So don't worry about tomorrow.

MATTHEW 6:32–34 NLT

Dear God of peace and rest and comfort,
Please bless this child from head to toe.
Make this special little one holy
in mind, body, and soul.
You have chosen Your children, and
You are faithful and good to them.
For this, we thank You and praise You.
Amen.

INSPIRED BY 1 THESSALONIANS 5:23–25

God Plus YOU = 2

Have you ever gotten lost? In a big store or in an unfamiliar neighborhood? Maybe in a new school? How did you feel?

Probably scared. Worried. And alone.

Did you know that you weren't *really* alone? God has promised us that He will always be with us, His children. Even when we are not children anymore. He will never leave us alone. You can talk to Him anytime. When you feel scared and alone, you *should* talk to Him, because He is right by your side. He can take away those lonely feelings.

Of course, God is not just for emergencies. You can pick up a Bible or storybook and read about Him whenever you want. You can sing songs about Him. You can even sing *to* Him—morning, noon, or night.

Isn't it a great feeling to know that even when we feel alone, we are not really alone? Thank God for that!

The LORD is with me; I will not be afraid.

PSALM 118:6

Jesus up in heaven high
Far above the dark night sky
Look on us with loving eyes.
Guard us, loving Jesus.
Snug and warm and so well fed,
Tucked all safely in our beds,
Come and kiss our sleepy heads.
Be near us, loving Jesus.

Remember the Chicken Pox!

Have you ever heard the saying, "Here comes trouble"?

It is always a good idea to avoid trouble when we see it coming our way. However, sometimes there is just no hiding from it. Trouble can be like a sudden rainstorm that hits when you have no umbrella or shelter. There's no way to keep from getting wet.

But when it comes to trouble, God has good news for us: No matter what kind of trouble comes into our lives, He can turn that trouble into something good. That doesn't mean the trouble itself is good; it's what happens *because* of the trouble that matters.

Think of it this way: Have you—or a brother, sister, or friend—ever had the chicken pox? If so, you know they are no fun. They are itchy and annoying. They can almost drive a kid crazy! However, getting those pesky pox once means that you will most likely never, ever get them again. In doctor-talk, you are *immune* to chicken pox. That's why some kids get a shot called a vaccine, to help them avoid chicken pox.

So the next time you fight with troubles, think of chicken pox. Like chicken pox, trouble is no fun when we are in the middle of it. But we should hold on to hope with all of our strength. Eventually, the good is going to outshine the bad! And you are going to leave your troubles behind and be a stronger little person because of what you have gone through. That's a promise from God!

We know that God causes everything to work together for the good of those who love God and are called according to his purpose for them.

Romans 8:28 NLT

17

Speak, Lord, for we long to hear You,
Speak peace to our anxious souls,
And help us to feel that all our ways
Are under Your wise control;
That You who care for the lily,
And heed the sparrows' fall,
Shall gently lead Your little ones:
For You made and love them all.

AUTHOR UNKNOWN

Telling Temptation "No!"

Let's say you visit a friend's house and you see a quarter lying in a dark corner. You might feel a little drop of temptation to sneak over and pick up that quarter.

Now, imagine that you see a one-hundred-dollar bill resting in that same dark corner. That "little drop" of temptation might turn into a whole ocean! Temptations come in lots of shapes and sizes, and no person is temptation-proof. What's more, probably everyone you know has given in to temptation at one time or another. Even moms and dads. Even preachers and Sunday school teachers! It is part of being human.

But here is good news: With practice—and with God's help— you can get better and better at saying "NO!" to temptations of all kinds. We can always ask God for the strength to fight temptation, and then we can practice putting that strength into action. As we do this, we improve our temptation-busting skills. Saying no to temptation is kind of like mastering a sport or a musical instrument or the multiplication tables or a dance routine. The more you do it, the better you get at it.

Here's more good news about temptation. God has promised that He will never give us more temptation than we can handle. Temptation might be really, really hard to fight, but not impossible. Especially with God's help.

Remember, too, that even heroes of the Bible, like David and Samson and Paul, struggled with temptation. Sometimes they won; sometimes they lost. Fortunately, God loves us no matter what. He just asks that we keep trying. And that we keep praying to Him for the wisdom and the will-power to do the right thing.

Don't be afraid, for I am with you. Don't be discouraged, for I am your God. I will strengthen you and help you. I will hold you up with my victorious right hand.

ISAIAH 41:10 NLT

And now to him who can keep you on your feet,
standing tall in his bright presence,
fresh and celebrating–to our one God,
our only Savior...Jesus Christ, our Master,
be glory, majesty, strength and rule...
now, and to the end of all time. Yes!

JUDE 1:24–25 MSG

Helpful Crocodiles

Crocodiles do not know how to eat with spoons, knives, and forks. (This is one of the many, many reasons that you should *not* invite a crocodile to dinner with your family.)

This lack of skill with spoons and such is a problem for crocs—apart from making them bad dinner guests. They sometimes have lots of trouble holding on to their food when they eat. (Have you noticed that crocodile "hands" are kind of fat and stubby?)

But the crocs have figured out a way to solve their problem. One crocodile will politely hold a chunk of wildebeest or zebra for another croc, so that he or she can take a nice big bite without dropping dinner on the ground, or in the water.

Crocs help each other with small snacks too. They will line up all the way across a stream so that no fish can get through. A fish will try to dodge one croc—only to swim right into the mouth of another!

If big, mean crocodiles can help each other, shouldn't we people do the same? After all, serving others isn't that hard. It doesn't mean you have to save someone's life or give him all your money and toys. It can be as simple as holding a door for someone. Even smiling at someone or sharing a snack or giving a compliment is a way of serving.

Have you ever seen a friend having a hard time and felt the urge to help him or her? That urge was probably God, encouraging you to serve someone. To put someone's needs ahead of your own.

Just don't try to help a crocodile eat. Leave that job for another croc!

Serve one another in love.

Galatians 5:13 nlt

May _____ do good things, in good ways.
Big things and small things. At all times.
To all kinds of people.
Now, and forever.
Amen.

One Tough Question!

Here's a tough question for you: what can you do to make God stop loving you?

If you answered, "Nothing!" you are exactly right.

Absolutely nothing will make God love you less. Yes, God can feel disappointed or sad when we make bad choices or act mean to someone, but He does *not* feel less love for us. When we make mistakes, we don't have to do a bunch of stuff to get back on God's good side. *Good* is the only kind of side God has. He doesn't have a bad side.

God wants to forgive you when you do something wrong. In fact, He is eager to forgive you. He doesn't want you to go around feeling guilty. He loves you even more than you can understand.

Should you try to make parents, teachers, and others proud of you? And to make God proud? Sure. But you don't have to earn the love of anyone who truly cares about you. You are loved just for being you! That's God's kind of love!

As a mother comforts her child, so will I comfort you.

Isaiah 66:13

Good night! Good night!
Far flies the light;
But still God's love
Shall shine above,
Making all bright,
Good night! Good night!

Victor Hugo

Prayer Power

Long before the first telephone or desktop computer or laptop or smartphone was invented, people were using the most amazing form of communication that will ever be invented.

This method always works, no matter where a person is. And it is completely free.

What are we talking about?

Prayer.

Prayer allows us to stay connected to God, all the time, any time! You can talk to God in prayer, no matter what you are doing. You can pray in the middle of a soccer game, in the middle of a math test, or even when you are brushing your teeth. You can pray out loud or just in your head, with your thoughts. And even if your only thought is *Aaaaargh*, you can share that with God. He understands

when you're so mad that you feel like throwing one of your toys across the room—even if you cannot put it into words!

Can you imagine being able to talk with your smartest teacher, your most caring grown-up, and your very best friend—all at once? You can do that! Just pray to God.

Never stop praying.

1 THESSALONIANS 5:17 NLT

No more time to run and play,
Now it's time to stop and pray.
Dear God, keep me through the night,
In Your arms please hold me tight.
Help me, Lord, to love You more,
than I have ever loved before.
When I work and when I play,
Be with me each night and day.

Sticking to It

On a cold February day, a small snail started climbing her way up a tall apple tree. The snail crawled very, very slowly, only a few inches every hour or so. When the snail was only a little way up the tree, a worm stuck its head out of a crack in the tree bark.

"You are wasting your time, silly snail," the worm said. "And you are wasting your energy. It is only February; there are no apples on this tree!"

The snail looked at the worm for a moment. Then she continued her climb. As she inched up the tree, she called back to the worm, "I know it is only February *now*, but by the time I get near the top of this tree, it will be summer. By the time I finish my climb, the apples will be there!"

The snail in this little story had something called *perseverance*. Have you heard that word before? Some people call perseverance "stick-to-it-ness." You have probably shown perseverance, even if the word is strange and new to you. If you have ever practiced really hard at a sport or with a musical instrument and gotten pretty good, that's perseverance.

If you have studied and studied for a test and earned a good grade, that's perseverance. Even if you have eaten every last vegetable on your plate so you could have dessert, that, too, is perseverance. (Especially if one of the vegetables was cauliflower—yuck!)

Developing stick-to-it-ness is God's way of helping us get through challenges so that we can feel good about working hard and being rewarded for that hard work. Perseverance is also the way God gets us ready for harder challenges—and greater rewards—in the future.

So let's not allow ourselves to get fatigued
doing good. At the right time we will
harvest a good crop if we don't give up, or quit.

GALATIANS 6:9 MSG

Dear God, I pray that You will bless this child with a love that has deep, deep roots—roots like a strong tree. Bless _____, too, with the power to understand the wonderful love of Your Son Jesus. A love that is as deep as the ocean and as tall as a mountain.

INSPIRED BY EPHESIANS 3:17–19

Way to Obey!

OBEY is probably not your favorite word. It can be hard to obey—
especially when there are so many people for a kid to obey: parents,
grandparents, teachers, coaches, pastors, babysitters, and maybe
even a bossy big brother or sister!

You might not feel like it is fun to obey, but please keep in mind
that it takes a lot of strength to obey. It takes patience too. Obeying
often means putting the right thing ahead of the fun thing. It means
doing something when we don't feel like it. Like going to bed when
we might not feel the least bit tired. Like saying "I'm sorry" for
yelling at someone—when we feel like saying, "You deserved to be
yelled at!"

But in the long run, obeying leads to a better life. It helps us stay
out of trouble. It teaches us respect for others. And it can help us set
a good example for other kids. Obedience is one of God's tools to
help you live a better and happier life.

Anyone who hears these teachings of mine is like a wise person who built his house on solid rock. Rains poured down, rivers flooded, and winds beat against that house. But it did not fall because it was built on solid rock.

MATTHEW 7:24–25 CEV

May I live each day through the strength of Jesus.
Lord, shield me today against all that is wrong.
Jesus, be with me,
Behind me, inside my heart, and beneath me,
Above me, on my right, and on my left.
When I lie down and when I rise up.
May Jesus be in every eye that sees me,
and in every ear that hears me.

INSPIRED BY A PRAYER OF ST. PATRICK

Heaven:
The Happiest Place in the World

What is heaven like? That is a hard question to answer, but picture your best day on earth—with all your dreams coming true—then multiply that by about a gazillion. Then multiply *that* by another gazillion or so. Then you might, *might* have some idea of how awesome heaven is. In other words, your room in heaven will not have your favorite candy in a jar on your dresser. It will have a candy way, way *better* than your favorite candy in a jar on the dresser!

In the past few years, a few people who got very sick or badly hurt have written books about how they died and went to heaven for a few minutes. Then they came back to life here on earth. All these people saw that heaven is so wonderful that it is hard to put into words!

We do know that one of the best things about heaven is that our earthly bodies—which can get sick, tired, or hurt—will be replaced by a heavenly body. Kind of like a super-hero body, only better. It will be sick-proof, and it will never get old or tired!

Our loving God gives us lots of things to look forward to on earth—Christmas, summer vacation, sleepovers with friends, and our birthdays. But heaven is what we can look forward to most. Because heaven is the home of God and all those who love Him! And heaven has a place just for you!

Praise be to the God and Father of our Lord Jesus Christ! In his great mercy he has given us new birth into a living hope through the resurrection of Jesus Christ from the dead, and into an inheritance that can never perish, spoil or fade. This inheritance is kept in heaven for you, who through faith are shielded by God's power.

1 PETER 1:3–5

For flowers that bloom about our feet,
Father, we thank You.
For tender grass so fresh and sweet,
Father, we thank You.
For the song of bird and hum of bee,
For the glory we will someday see,
Father in heaven, we thank You.

INSPIRED BY RALPH WALDO EMERSON

Giving Thanks for Thanksgiving

Do you like Thanksgiving? What is your favorite part? Pumpkin pie? Seeing family you love? Playing football in the yard? A few days away from school?

Did you know that America's first president, George Washington, was the first person to suggest having a national holiday of thanks? Unfortunately, not enough people liked President Washington's idea, so there was no Thanksgiving Day during his lifetime.

Many, many years later, President Abraham Lincoln tried to revive Washington's idea. President Lincoln was especially grateful for the end of the Civil War, and he wanted the last Thursday of each November to be set aside for people to give thanks for all of God's blessings.

Sadly, President Lincoln did not succeed in establishing this national holiday before he died. In fact, it took almost eighty years after Mr. Lincoln's death for Thanksgiving Day to become a national holiday. Finally, in 1941, it was declared that the fourth Thursday of each November would be Thanksgiving Day.

Thanksgiving Day isn't a very old holiday, but for a long, long time, people have realized that it is important to give thanks. Of all God's blessings, which ones are YOU most thankful for?

Give thanks to the LORD, for he is good!
His faithful love endures forever.

PSALM 107:1 NLT

Thank You for a world so sweet,
Thank You for the food I eat,
Thank You for the songs we sing,
Thank You, God, for everything.

With Love Like Glue, God's Stuck on YOU!

You are full of laminin. Absolutely full of it. And you should be grateful for all that laminin inside you. If you didn't have this stuff, you would be falling apart right now. And I don't mean getting mad or sad and crying and shrieking. Not that kind of falling apart. We are talking *actual* falling apart. Kind of like melting all over the place!

Laminin is a very important protein in your body. In fact, it is known as the body's Super Glue. It helps hold your muscles, your skin, your eyes—all of you—together.

God's love is a lot like laminin. It fills us up. It lives in every single cell of our bodies, and it sticks to us like the world's strongest glue! Even when we are sad, or someone has been mean to us, God's love inside of us helps us feel better and makes us strong.

God loves you to pieces—and all of your pieces are held together by the strength of His forever love! Let this good news stick with you all of your life!

And I am convinced that nothing can ever separate
us from God's love...nothing in all creation will
ever be able to separate us from the love of God
that is revealed in Christ Jesus our Lord.

ROMANS 8:38–39 NLT

God made the world so big and grand
Filled with blessings
From His hand.
He made the sky
So high and blue,
And this special child too!

A Big Hairy Deal

Have you ever tried to count every single hair on your head? What number did you come up with?

If you are a redhead, you have about 90,000 hairs. If your hair is brown or black, you have about 110,000. And if you are blond, you have a whopping 140,000 hairs sprouting from your scalp!

God knows the *exact* number of hairs on your head. He loves you so much that it's important to Him to know even the little things about you. And He knows the big things too.

One of the Bible writers said, "You know me inside and out, you know every bone in my body; You know exactly how I was made,

bit by bit, how I was sculpted from nothing into something. Like an open book, you watched me grow" (Psalm 139:15–16 MSG). What does this verse mean? God loves you. From the bottom of your feet to the top of your head—including your hair!

The very hairs on your head are all numbered.
So don't be afraid; you are...valuable to him.

LUKE 12:7 NLT

Now I lay me down to sleep,
I pray thee, Lord, Your child to keep;
Your love to guard me through the night
And wake me in the morning light.

No Need to Fear

Have you ever woken up in the middle of the night and found your own bedroom to be a scary place? Did strange shapes, shadows, and sounds make you freeze in fear? Isn't it weird how a familiar place can be transformed into a haunted house?

But what happened when you, or some kind big person, turned on the lights? Those scary shadows disappeared. The once-strange shapes became familiar again. The "troll" crouching in the corner was just a mound of dirty laundry. The "ghost" hovering in the closet was just a coat on a hanger.

And the sounds—the clicks, groans, and rumbles—were not so scary in the light, were they?

That's the way God's hope is. Like light, it floods into your world, warming and lighting up everything. It chases away fear.

Hope is a gift that God loves to give you. He enjoys surprising you by fulfilling your hopes—and then giving you even more than you could have *imagined* asking for.

So the next time you are scared or uncertain, ask God for His gift of hope. Let Him give your heart a hug—a hug that says, "I love you. Everything is going to be okay. Have hope."

> *God will help you overflow with hope in him*
> *through the Holy Spirit's power within you.*
>
> ROMANS 15:13 TLB

Bless the four corners of this house,
And the foundation be blessed,
And bless the floors and bless the dinner table,
And bless each place of rest.
And bless the door that opens wide,
to old friends and new,
Bless each shining window
That lets Your sunshine in;
And bless the roof over our heads
And every sturdy wall—
The peace of humankind, the peace of God,
The peace of Your love on us all.

INSPIRED BY A TRADITIONAL CHRISTIAN BLESSING

Your Own Personal Angels

Angels are the stars of many Bible adventures.

Let's consider the first-ever Easter, for example. On the day Jesus rose from the dead, angels greeted some people who came to Jesus' tomb. These people wanted to honor Jesus and remember what a great person He was. And they wanted to comfort each other, because they were so sad Jesus was gone.

But instead of finding Jesus lying dead in a grave, these people saw angels instead. These angels greeted the sad people with the happy news that Jesus had risen from the dead, showing the world that He has power over death—and the power to forgive people for everything they have done wrong!

By the way, Christian legends tells us that the angels were so happy when Jesus rose from the dead that they played a game of "catch" with the huge stone that sealed His tomb. That stone weighed about two thousand pounds, about as much as your family car! They tossed it around like a ball.

Did you know angels are really, really strong? And aren't you glad that you have strong guardian angels like this watching over YOU? The Bible promises us, "The angel of the LORD encamps around those who fear him, and he delivers them" (Psalm 34:7).

"See that you do not despise one of these little ones. For I tell you that their angels in heaven always see the face of my Father in heaven."

MATTHEW 18:10

When at night I go to sleep
fourteen angels watch do keep.
Two my head are guarding,
two my feet are guiding,
two are at my right hand,
two are at my left hand,
two who warmly cover,
two who over me hover,
and two to whom is given,
to guide my steps to heaven.

GERMAN BLESSING

The Way of Yahweh

Yahweh (Yah-way) is the Hebrew word for God. When Bible heroes like Abraham, David, and Moses prayed to God, they called him Yahweh.

The Bible tells us all about Yahweh's big plan for the world. Sometimes, this was a hard plan to carry out. For example, it was very, very painful for Yahweh to watch His beloved Son Jesus die. (Think of how you feel when you watch your mom or dad, friend, or brother or sister get badly hurt or really sick.)

God's suffering was extra-hard because He had the power to stop Jesus from being killed. But He knew that if Jesus didn't take the punishment for all of people's sins, the people wouldn't be able to handle that punishment by themselves. So, painful as it was, God allowed Jesus to suffer so that all of us can have eternal life and be

forgiven for all we have done wrong. Let's take time tonight to thank Yahweh for being willing to let His Son die for us.

God loved the world so much that he gave his
one and only Son so that whoever believes in
him may not be lost, but have eternal life.

JOHN 3:16 NCV

O, Yahweh,
Be to this child like the evergreen tree,
shelter _____ in Your shade,
and bless this child again and again,
like the warm and gentle rain.
The rain that gives life
to all You have made.

INSPIRED BY HOSEA 14:4–8

Doctor Robot Will See You Now...

Imagine your next appointment with the doctor or dentist. You go to your appointment, expecting to see the same man or woman who usually helps you feel better and fixes things that need to be fixed—whether it's teeth, toes, tongue, or tonsils.

But this time, something is different. Instead of meeting a person with "Doctor" in front of his or her name, you meet a robot! A robot holding some medical tools and ready to go to work... on you!

Believe it or not, this kind of thing could really happen. In some places, it already is. Robotic surgery is one of the big changes

happening in the world of doctors and medicine. Robots are fixing damaged hearts. Robots are transplanting kidneys. Robots are even removing cancer from people's bodies.

Now, as you are probably thinking, the robots are not doing all this stuff on their own. Human doctors are still in charge. These doctors use computers that remote-control the robot, which has medical tools attached to its robot arms. Kind of like how you use a video-game controller or computer keys to control a video game.

What does all of this have to do with you? Well, you are kind of like those robot doctors. Really. Here's how: The Bible says that YOU are God's hands. Did you know that? Just as a doctor chooses to use a robot to get some of His work done, God has chosen people like you to "be His hands" to do good things here on earth.

What an honor it is to be called God's hands! We should all work really hard to use our hands to do good things!

Never walk away from someone who deserves help; your hand is God's hand for that person.

PROVERBS 3:27 MSG

Sleep my little one.
Through the wind and through the rain.
Through the passing of the night.
Until we see God's sun again.
And when the new day dawns...
Do good, my little one.
Be God's hands, and show God's love.
To all people who need kindness.
Whenever you have the chance.

Just for Being YOU

Lots of people love you. You know that, right? Have you ever thought about what makes them love you? Is it your singing voice? Your talent at sports? Your brain? Your good looks? Your kindness? The great jokes and riddles you tell?

Your family and friends probably appreciate things like these, but the real reason you are loved is this: You are *you*! That's right—you are loved just for being who you are! This is the way God wants us to love one another. With God, love just comes naturally, and He can help us learn to love the way He does.

The Bible tells us that God *is* love. That means He loves us even when we are not acting very lovable. This is an important thing to remember, especially when we have done something wrong. God does not love us because of how good we are. He loves us because of how good HE is!

God is love, and anyone who doesn't love
others has never known him.

1 JOHN 4:8 CEV

Loving God,
Thank You for caring for this
child's journey through life.
As _____ faces what lies ahead,
may these eyes be focused on You.
May You be at this one's side always,
even when he/she is not so little anymore.

Putting Your Gifts to Work

Imagine that you will get a huge package on your birthday or Christmas. Any chance you would let that beautiful package sit there for days and days? Any chance you'd never open it?

Well, God is the greatest gift-giver of all time. He has given each of His children—you included—wonderful gifts. The gift of being kind. The gift of being able to fix a broken toy. A talent for telling stories. A smile that makes everyone happy. The talent to draw amazing pictures or create some other work of art. If we use our gifts wisely, we can help people around us, and make God so happy. He loves seeing His gifts put to use.

Putting your heaven-sent gifts to work is one of the best things you can do in life. Doing the things God created you to do helps you feel good inside, and it makes you feel closer to the One who gave you your talents in the first place. Few things in life are as beautiful as Creator and creation (you!) working together!

Do not neglect your gift.

1 TIMOTHY 4:14

Dear Lord, who gives us life,
please give us, every day,
hearts full of thankfulness
for all You have given us!

INSPIRED BY WILLIAM SHAKESPEARE

Pizza, Peanut Butter, or *Sushi*?

What is your favorite food in the whole world? Pizza? Chocolate ice cream? Peanut butter and jelly sandwiches? Sushi? (Okay, probably not sushi.)

Our bodies need food to give us energy and keep us healthy and strong. But did you know that your soul needs food too? Without this "soul food," we can't grow as children of God. We might have trouble knowing right from wrong. We might have trouble treating other people the way we want to be treated.

We can divide soul food into four basic groups, like we sometimes do with regular food:

Bible food. You can get this food by reading the Bible or a Bible storybook or a Sunday school lesson. Videos and TV shows (like *Veggie Tales*) can also be a fun way to learn lessons from the Bible.

Prayer food. Think of prayer like an all-day snack. You can pray about big things, little things, and everything in between! No matter what we pray or when we pray, God is there listening to us.

Worship food. We worship God when we sing to Him. We can worship Him when we pray. You can even write God a poem or song! And when you do good things, that is another way to worship God.

Fellowship food. Fellowship is simply being around other people who love God and want to serve Him. This can be with kids your own age—in Sunday school or children's church. Or it can be with people older than you, or younger than you. Fellowship helps people learn from each other and cheer each other up. Have you ever been on a sports team or in a band or choir or club? Then you know how fun it is to be part of a team, all trying for the same goal. It is the same way with God's people.

Once you have enjoyed a good taste of soul food, you will never want to let your soul get hungry again. And there is no reason to. God has provided a big buffet that will never run out of good stuff.

*The living God...provides you with plenty
of food and fills your hearts with joy.*

ACTS 14:15, 17 NIV

For each new morning with its light,
Father, we thank You,
For rest and shelter through the night,
Father, we thank You,
For health and food, for love and friends,
For everything Your goodness sends,
Father in heaven, we thank You.

INSPIRED BY RALPH WALDO EMERSON

A Reason to Sing

After learning that she would give birth to God's son, Mary was so happy that she made up a song. (See Luke 1:46–55.) Her song begins, "My soul glorifies the Lord and my spirit rejoices in God my Savior. . . . From now on, all generations will call me blessed, for the Mighty One has done great things for me—holy is his name."

Whenever you sing a song about Jesus, remember to sing it with all your heart, the way Mary did. Put all your feelings and all your energy into it.

Hey, would you like to try to write a song to Jesus, just as Mary did? You can do it. And if you need a little help, you know you can find a grown-up to help you. Perhaps even the grown-up who is reading to you right now!

Mary said,
I'm bursting with God-news; I'm dancing the song of my
Savior God. God took one good look at me, and look what
happened—I'm the most fortunate woman on earth!

LUKE 1:46–47 MSG

Dear heavenly Father,
Make this precious one's life a song.
A song with words that comfort the sad.
A song with melodies and harmonies
that give hope to discouraged people.
A song that makes the happy people even happier.
Amen.

Sins in the Sea's Bottom

Have you ever held your breath and tried to touch the bottom of a swimming pool? Did you make it?

Well, have you ever wondered where you could find the deepest water in the whole world?

Out in the Pacific Ocean, near the island of Guam, you will find the Mariana Trench—which is kind of like a giant ditch at the bottom of the ocean's floor. The Mariana Trench is almost seven miles deep. You could put huge Mount Everest, the world's highest mountain, in this trench, and the very tip-top would be more than a mile underwater!

If you wanted to visit the Mariana Trench, you would need a specially built submarine to handle the great pressure of the water—otherwise, you could get squished like a grape! The vehicles that explore the Mariana Trench have to be super strong, and the people in them have to be really patient. It takes about five hours to get from the ocean surface to the bottom of the trench.

In the Bible, we are promised that God forgives our sins, and He sinks them to the bottom of the ocean (Micah 7:19). So, the next time you tell God you are sorry for something you've done, imagine Him taking your sin and burying it way, way down at the bottom of the Mariana Trench. That's how far away God takes our sins from us. He doesn't hold our sins against us. He buries them deep, deep, deep at the ocean's bottom. They are forgiven and forgotten.

You'll sink our sins to the bottom of the ocean.

MICAH 7:19 MSG

Loving God,
Thank You for the plans You have for this child.
Plans to prosper, not to harm.
Plans for hope and a big, bright future.
You will hear his/her prayers.
You will always be there for _____
For this, we thank and praise You!

INSPIRED BY JEREMIAH 29:11–13

Talking Donkeys, Walking Skeletons, and a Bush on Fire

Just how far will God go to talk with His people? Let's look at some examples:

When God wanted to grab Moses' attention, He spoke to him through a bright burning bush.

When God wanted to help his prophet Balaam make the right choice, Balaam's donkey *talked*, delivering an important message from God!

When God wanted his prophet Ezekiel to understand the difference between old life and new life, He turned a valley of old, dried-up bones into living people!

And when a man named Jonah (do you know him?) tried to ignore God's orders, God sent a giant fish to swallow Jonah and then spit him out—right where God wanted him to be.

These are all amazing stories that show us how much God wants to grab our attention and communicate with us. However, the most amazing example of all is Jesus. When God wanted to express His love for all people, He sent His beloved Son Jesus to heal the sick, to die for our sins, and to show us how to live. What a wonderful message—and what a wonderful way to deliver it!

The Lord is watching his children, listening to their prayers.

1 PETER 3:12 TLB

May the Lord your God lift you high.
May you be blessed in the big, busy city
or the quiet small town.
May God bless the work of your
hands and your brain.
May you be blessed in your home,
and far, far beyond your home.
May your enemies be defeated.
May they run away in fear because
you have God on your side.
May the Lord make you holy.
May His blessings sprinkle gently on you
like refreshing spring rain.

INSPIRED BY DEUTERONOMY 28:1–12

Thank God for Your Pod!

You might have heard of a pack of wolves or a herd of sheep—but what do you call a group of dolphins? Groups of dolphins are called *pods*, and we can learn a thing or two from these dolphin pods. First of all, dolphin pods have a lot of fun with each other. They splash and play and perform tricks to entertain each other, kind of like a bunch of kids in a swimming pool.

More important, though, dolphins take care of each other. If a dolphin gets hurt or sick, two other dolphins put their fins under their friend and bring him to water's surface so that he can breathe. (Maybe you know that dolphins breathe air, just like people. They cannot breathe underwater like fish.)

Just as God provides dolphin pods that care for one another, He has given you lots and lots of people to care for you. Family, friends, teachers, and people at church. Isn't it a great blessing to travel through life with so many people who support you and care for you—in good times and in hard times? Don't forget to thank God for your pod!

Friends come and friends go, but a true friend sticks by you like family.

PROVERBS 18:24 MSG

Dear God, thank You for surrounding me with people who love me so much. Their love reminds me of how much You love me too!

Ashlee and the Burnt Toys

When you're six years old, toys are a big deal, right? So when Ashlee Smith's toys were destroyed in a house fire a few years ago, she was very, very sad.

Two years later, when a fire in California destroyed 254 homes, Ashlee's own sad memories came rushing back to her. She thought of all the kids whose homes had burned down. She knew what they were feeling. And she knew just how to help.

Ashlee began collecting toys to give to kids who'd lost everything they owned in the fire. "I wanted to help the little victims in a big way," she said.

After she provided toys for the California kids, Ashlee kept on going. Today "Ashlee's Toy Closet," and its now thirteen-year-old founder, continue to provide toys, books, and clothing to children affected by fires and other disasters.

Ashlee turned something that hurt her into something that helped others. She thought about her own painful experience and used what she learned from it to comfort other kids. That's exactly what the Bible says God will help each of us do. Second Corinthians 1:4 says, "He comes alongside us when we go through hard times, and before we know it, he brings us alongside someone else who is going through hard times so that we can be there for that person, just as God was there for us" (MSG).

The LORD is close to the brokenhearted,
and he saves those whose spirits have been crushed.

PSALM 34:18 NCV

May our loving Jesus pour love
on you—so much love
that it fills up your life and splashes
on everyone around you!

INSPIRED BY 1 THESSALONIANS 3:12

Get in the Swim of Things!

"What that kid just did oughta be against the law!" a man shouted. The man was talking about eleven-year-old Thomas Gregory. The man was right.

What Thomas did was shocking, but it also set a world record that will never be broken. After Thomas completed his amazing adventure, new rules were made. No other eleven-year-old could even try to do what Thomas did. From that moment on, a boy or girl would have to be at least sixteen to even try it.

What, exactly, did Thomas Gregory do one early September day several years ago?

He swam through raw sewage. He dodged toxic oil slicks and the painful stings of jellyfish. He fought angry waves as tall as giants. He paddled his way around hungry, swirling whirlpools that enjoy nothing more than swallowing untrained swimmers. He punched through the pain of cramps in his arms, legs, and back. And he did it all in water so cold that it felt like his blood was turning to a slushie.

Eleven-year-old Thomas Gregory swam all the way from France to England, knifing his way across roughly twenty-five miles of angry waters known as the English Channel. The feat has killed its share of strong adult swimmers. All told, only about one in ten grown-ups who try to swim across the Channel can do it. Even some Olympic champion swimmers have tried and not made it.

Thomas, who could still order from the kids menu at local restaurants, completed his swim in just under twelve hours, breaking his age-group's record by almost three hours! In fact, he crossed the Channel in about half the time of the first grown-up who made the swim. And that man used a special wet suit, which were later outlawed.

Thomas's secret? He was determined. He wanted to conquer what many people consider the ultimate endurance challenge. That's what kept him going through eight-hour training sessions in cold, cold waters as he got ready to face the Channel.

"I wanted to do this," he explained. "It was my goal, and nothing was going to stop me."

What about you? You don't need to swim across a huge body of water. But just imagine where trying really, really hard can take you. You can do amazing stuff when you try hard...and pray hard. And don't let doubters discourage you.

Just be like Thomas Gregory and show them that they're all wet.

Anything is possible if a person believes.

MARK 9:23 NLT

May our Lord Jesus Christ Himself
and God our Father cheer you on
and strengthen you in every
good thing you do and say.
God loves you, and through His grace
He gives you a good hope
and the kind of help that goes on forever.

INSPIRED BY 2 THESSALONIANS 2:16–17

Battling a Best Buddy

Have you ever had to compete against your best friend? That's what happened to two girls named Esther and Kay. Esther and Kay had been best buds since they were very young. One activity they enjoyed doing together was the martial art Tae Kwon Do, a form of karate. They both became experts at Tae Kwon Do. By the time they were grown-ups, the two friends were so good that they tried out for the United States Olympic team.

Both Esther and Kay did well in the Olympic Trials. Soon, they were scheduled to compete against each other for a spot on the Olympic team. Making the team was a dream they both shared. Unfortunately, Kay had dislocated her kneecap earlier in the tournament. She could barely stand up, let alone do any karate moves.

When the time came for the two friends to compete, Esther did something amazing. She forfeited the match. She said she would not fight her hurt friend, even if it meant giving up a spot on the Olympic team!

When the Bible tells us that love is not selfish, this is what it means. Love means thinking of others before we think of ourselves. This is not always easy to do, but the selfless love that Esther showed Kay is the kind of love that makes us champions in God's eyes!

Whenever you are able, do good to people who need help.

PROVERBS 3:27 NCV

Dear Jesus, oh, how well You know me,
Every step I take, You show me.
When I rise and when I rest,
My loving Jesus knows me best.
As I walk or sit or stand,
You will hold me in Your hand.
When I don't know what to do or say,
I know You will show the way.

Small Moments Matter Big-Time

Magic moments. You've had them. Chugging a cold bubbling soda after a hot day of playing or working outside. Holding Mom or Dad's hand on a walk to the ice cream shop. Seeing that familiar smile flash across your best friend's face when you meet up to go play. Hearing a grown-up mention *your* name when thanking God for His blessings.

Every moment like these is a gift to you from God. Our Creator sends these gifts to remind us that His supply of love and kindness will never run out. And because of this, we should always be thankful.

These gifts also remind us to keep our eyes, minds, and hearts open for the blessings—both large and small—that await us in the future. Who knows what magic moments will fill our hearts with laughter and make us want to shout with joy?

God will load your world with blessings, large and small. Take time to enjoy them all.

He will yet fill your mouth with laughter
and your lips with shouts of joy.

JOB 8:21

Generous God,
I will know You will surely bless this child,
with more joys than there are stars in the sky
or sands on the seashore.
This little one will be blessed
for loving You and obeying You.

INSPIRED BY GENESIS 22:15–18

Jesus' All-You-Can-Eat Buffet

Have you heard the Bible story about how Jesus fed more than five thousand people, using just the lunch provided by one small boy? (This story can be found in the sixth chapter of John's Gospel, if you need to refresh your memory.)

You might remember that this boy's lunch was five loaves of bread and two fish. But the "loaves" in this story were not like the big ones you find at the grocery store today. They were about the size of a Twinkie. And the fish were little, not the kind of prize fish you might see a fisherman posing with.

The boy's lunch was pretty small. Barely enough to feed a kid like you. When Jesus first asked the boy to share his food, that kid must have thought, "But, Jesus, there's not enough to give all these people even one single crumb of food!"

But, somehow, Jesus used the boy's tiny gift to meet the needs of hungry thousands! Like that boy, you might sometimes feel that you do not have very much to offer our Lord. But that's not true. Jesus can take even the smallest gift and do amazing things with it. That's why it is so important to give what we have—and not worry about what we don't have.

If you are really eager to give, then it isn't important how much you have to give. God wants you to give what you have, not what you haven't.

2 CORINTHIANS 8:12 TLB

Jesus, nourishing bread of life,
Jesus, refreshing water of life,
Jesus, Lord of all life, be with this dear child.
Jesus, Lord of love, hold this
child close to Your heart.

INSPIRED BY AN AFRICAN BLESSING

You Against a Giant?

Imagine that you have to fight a giant. This giant is almost ten feet tall, and the armor he wears weighs more than you do. He has deadly weapons, including a huge spear, whose tip alone weighs fifteen pounds.

You, on the other hand, have no armor. And your only weapon is a slingshot and five rocks. Does this sound like a fair fight to you?

But what if God was on your side, not the giant's? Then you just might load a rock in your slingshot and let it fly. That rock might smack the huge giant in the head. And he's toast!

As you have probably guessed, this story really happened many, many years ago. The kid with the slingshot was named David, and his giant enemy was named Goliath.

Now, you are probably not going to have to battle any ten-foot giants in your life, but life can bring giant-sized challenges. However, no matter what, God is going to be by your side, and He will give you whatever you need to win! That is one rock-solid promise.

I can do all things through Christ who strengthens me.

PHILIPPIANS 4:13 NKJV

May you live a life worthy of our Lord.
May you please Him in every way,
as you do good things and learn more
and more about God and His amazing Son.
May He give you strength and endurance.
May you give joyful thanks always to the One
who has let you enter the kingdom of light.

INSPIRED BY COLOSSIANS 1: 9–12

You: A Work of Art, and a Work of Heart!

Have you ever watched someone make a blanket or some clothes? If so, you might be familiar with words like sewing, knitting, crocheting, or quilting. In the Bible, it says that God knitted YOU together (Psalm 139).

Knitting is a carefully planned, step-by-step way to create something beautiful. That means that YOU are special! You were created by a Master Artist. His name is God. What's more, you weren't just created to be looked at and admired. You were created for a purpose. You were created to do good works that God has planned for you to do.

Yes, God made you carefully, and He made you lovingly. He created you to do special stuff. Some days, you might not feel smart enough, or strong enough or brave enough to do good things. But

you are! That is a promise from God. You are more than enough to accomplish everything God has planned for you!

You created my inmost being; you knit me together
in my mother's womb. I praise you because
I am fearfully and wonderfully made.

PSALM 139:13–14

Dear God of peace,
Please bless this child from head to toe.
Make this wonderful little person
holy in mind, body, and soul.
You have chosen Your children;
You have made them with great care,
and You are faithful and good to each one.
For this, we thank You and praise You.

INSPIRED BY 1 THESSALONIANS 5:23–25

The Wise Guy's One Wish

Have you ever wished really, really hard for something? What if you could wish for ANYTHING in the whole world—no matter what it cost?

If you could make a wish like that, what would you ask for?

Many, many years ago, a king got a once-in-a-lifetime offer just like the one we have been reading about. An offer from God Himself! This king's name was Solomon, and he was the son of the mighty giant-slayer David. God said to Solomon, "I will grant you one wish. Pick any gift you want, and I will give it to you."

Do you know what Solomon chose? It wasn't money, fame, or super-strength. It wasn't the ability to make himself invisible or to time-travel or to fly like a bird. Instead, Solomon chose wisdom. Really. Solomon wanted to be a smart king who would do a good job of leading his people. And without God's help, he was afraid he might do a bad job.

God was so happy with Solomon's choice that He made Solomon the wisest person of all time! Why was God happy? He knows that wisdom is precious, and He was delighted to see Solomon make such a good choice. Wisdom helps us make all kinds of smart decisions. Wisdom helps us know which words and actions are good—and which are not-so-good.

Did you know that you can ask for wisdom, just as Solomon did? God won't make you the wisest person in the world, but He will make you plenty wise enough to have a great life. If you ask God with a pure and humble heart, He will give you lots and lots of wisdom.

No one is like the wise person who can understand what things mean. Wisdom brings happiness; it makes sad faces happy.

ECCLESIASTES 8:1 NCV

God bless hill and stone and flower and tree,
From highest hill to deepest sea.
Place Your peace around our home.
Give us wisdom, as we roam.
Bless the earth and bless the sea,
God bless you, and God bless me!

INSPIRED BY AN OLD ENGLISH PRAYER

The Secret of Noel

Do you know the word NOEL? Pay attention this coming Christmas, and you will probably hear people saying "Noel"—maybe singing it too.

What does Noel mean, anyway? In France, across the ocean from North America, Noel is how the people say *Christmas*. Instead of shouting, "Merry Christmas," many French say, "Joyeaux Noel!"

Noel is a word that comes from shortening the French phrase *les bonnes nouvelles* (pronounced: lay bun new vell.) This means "the good news." The good news, in this case, is that Jesus came to earth to take away our sins. The good news is also that Jesus lives in the hearts of all people who love Him.

If Jesus lives in your heart, you know how good it feels to have Him living there. If you would like to invite Jesus into your heart, there are lots of people who can help you—including the person who is reading this book to you right now!

God assured us, "I'll never let you down,
never walk off and leave you."

HEBREWS 13:5 MSG

Jesus, tender shepherd, hear me;
Bless Your little lamb tonight.
Through darkness may Your love shine clearly
From midnight's chimes till morning light.

Eliab the Handsome

Who is your favorite movie or TV star or sports hero? Do you think he or she looks really good? Strong? Graceful? Confident? Handsome or beautiful?

There were no movies or TV shows or Super Bowls three thousand years ago, but if there were, a guy named Eliab would have been a big star. Eliab was the son of a man named Jesse, and he was the tallest and handsomest of all Jesse's sons.

When God decided that the nation of Israel needed a new king, he sent a man named Samuel to find someone worthy to wear the crown. Samuel's search took him to Jesse's house, and when he saw Eliab, he felt sure he had found the future king. After all, wouldn't God want a tall, strong, and handsome dude as king?

God had other ideas. He told Samuel to pick Eliab's littlest brother. A harp-playing shepherd kid named David. You see, Samuel was focusing on *outside* appearance, but God was much more concerned about what the future king was like on the inside. Did he have a good heart? Was he a man who would pray for wisdom and hope? Would he admit it when he made a mistake and try to be a better person because of it?

Have you heard the saying "Don't judge a book by its cover?" God feels this way about people. You might not feel like you are as tall and strong as you would like to be. You might not like everything about your outer appearance. But that is not how God sees you.

God looks at your beautiful heart, and you make Him so happy when you love other people. When you do this, you are more beautiful to God than you could ever imagine!

GOD told Samuel, "Looks aren't everything.
Don't be impressed with his [Eliab's] looks and stature....
GOD judges persons differently than humans do. Men
and women look at the face; GOD looks into the heart."

1 SAMUEL 16:7 MSG

May our God bless you and
take good care of you.
May He be kind to you and
do good things for you.
May He smile lovingly whenever He looks at you.
May He help you feel good inside
and give you peace.

INSPIRED BY NUMBERS 6:24–26

God Says, "No Sweat!"

God doesn't sweat. He doesn't get tired or get sore muscles. He never needs to take medicine. But what did He do after creating the whole world?

God rested. He took the time to stop working and enjoy His creation. If our all-powerful God took time to rest, doesn't that set an example for us humans?

We all need to rest once in a while. Even kids like you, who are full of energy! We need to rest our bodies, our minds, and our spirits. We need to take the time to be thankful to God for all of His blessings.

Chilling out and relaxing sometimes will help you to think about God's wonders and His blessings. His kindness to His children. Children just like you!

I will lie down and sleep in peace, for you alone, O LORD, make me dwell in safety.

PSALM 4:8

For rest and shelter through the night,
For the next morning and its light,
For health and food, for love and friends,
For every gift my Father sends,
We thank You, gracious Lord.

Bright Ideas

Have you ever counted how many lights are in your home? Do you know who first came up with the idea for the light bulb? If you said Thomas Edison, you are right!

Inventing the light bulb wasn't easy. In fact, Thomas Edison said he tried three thousand different ways to make a light bulb. But only two of them worked! That means Mr. Edison had to endure 2,998 goof-ups before he found success! Can you imagine how frustrated he must have been when bulb after bulb after bulb refused to work? But he kept going. He was determined and patient.

It is important to understand that we must *decide* to be patient and determined. It's not about how we feel. Sometimes we have to keep trying even when we don't feel like it.

I bet you have a lot of bright ideas. Ideas are one of God's gifts to us. But He wants us to be patient and determined as we put

those ideas into action. So always keep trying. Eventually, you'll see the light!

Whatever I have, wherever I am, I can make it through anything in the One who makes me who I am.

PHILIPPIANS 4:13 MSG

When I am scared and want to hide,
I know that You are by my side.
When I am lonely, You are near,
When I am sad, You bring me cheer.
You are with me everywhere
You promise me You'll always care
Know me, lead me, light my way,
Through every hour of every day,
Throughout my life, in all I do,
Keep me always close to You.

INSPIRED BY PSALM 139

Bites, Bruises, and Stings—Ouch!

When you get hurt, who do you run to? When you fall down? When a door slams on your finger? When a bug bites or stings you?

Isn't it great to have people to run to at times like these? Someone to wipe away your tears and take care of your ouchies?

Did you know that the Bible says that, someday, *God* will wipe away your tears? That's right—the hands that stretched out the heavens, sprinkled the stars across the sky, and molded the mountains will gently touch your cheek and lovingly brush away your tears forever. And when those tears disappear, so will whatever caused them in the first place!

Heaven is going to be a great place, with room for lots of stuff. But not *all* stuff. In heaven, there will be no room for tears.

God will wipe away every tear from their eyes.

REVELATION 21:4 NKJV

Angel of God, guardian dear,
We know God's love has placed you here.
Stand your guard at this bedside,
And through the night with love abide.
Angel of God, friend for years,
Calm all fears, dry all tears.

God Is for You!

Have you ever felt like someone was against you? Maybe a kid in your neighborhood or at school? Well, no matter who might be against you, take heart! God is on your side always. And always means right now, of course! He is thinking about you, helping you, and loving you, even as you are hearing these words!

God is a true friend. He loves you and comforts you even if you aren't doing all the right things. And even if your attitude toward Him is less than perfect. In other words, you don't have to earn God's love, and you cannot lose His love just because you do something wrong.

You have been created with a purpose in life—a purpose custom-made for your talents. And God is committed to seeing you fulfill your purpose. He isn't watching from far away. He is right beside you, cheering you on—and comforting you if things don't go well.

Yes, life can be hard sometimes. But not too hard. God is with you, and with Him by your side, it does not matter what or who is against you. You're gonna win!

The LORD God then said:
I will look for my sheep and take care of them myself.

EZEKIEL 34:11 CEV

Dear God, be with me every day,
In my work and in my play.
When I learn and when I pray
Please bless me, loving Father.

A Promise Made
Is a Promise Kept

Have you ever made a promise to someone? Did you keep that promise? Do you know that when Jesus came to earth, it was one way God kept a promise to His people? For many, many years, preachers told people that a Messiah (a Savior) would come one day and help them solve their problems. For example, seven hundred years before Jesus was born, a man named Isaiah revealed this promise about the Messiah:

"For to us a child is born, to us a son is given, and the government will be on his shoulders. And he will be called Wonderful Counselor, Mighty God, Everlasting Father, Prince of Peace" (Isaiah 9:6).

During His life, Jesus fulfilled this promise. He proved that He deserved all of those great names Isaiah called Him—and many, many more!

It is such a blessing to know that God and Jesus always keep their promises, and always fulfill the holy promises made *about* them.

Sing a new song to the Lord, for he has done wonderful deeds. His right hand has won a mighty victory; his holy arm has shown his saving power!

PSALM 98:1 NLT

Wonderful God of Promises,
All my life, Your hand has led me.
I know You are with me everywhere.
You have warmed and clothed and fed me.
So I thank You now in prayer.

Hide-and-Seek with God?

Do you like to play hide-and-seek? Are you good at it? Have you ever found such a good hiding place that no one could find you?

Well, if God were to play hide-and-seek with you, He could find you every time, because He is so smart and He can see everything. This is very good news. We are so blessed that God is always with us. This means that He can always hear our prayers. And it means that even when family and friends can't be near us, God can!

You are never, ever alone. That is really a good thing.

In hide-and-seek...and in life!

O LORD, you…*know everything about me.*
You know when I sit down or stand up.
You know my thoughts even when I'm far away.
You see me when I travel and when I rest at home.
You know everything I do.

PSALM 139:1–3 NLT

Sleep, my little one.
May God in safety your heart keep.
My little loved one,
sleep, sleep, sleep.

AUTHOR UNKNOWN

Pick Up a Penny—Possibly?

There's a penny on the sidewalk. Do you stoop down to pick it up? That depends on how much it's worth to you. If you're feeling rich, why bother with that little coin? What's it going to get you? One piece of bubble gum? Not even.

But what if your pockets are empty? What if you haven't eaten since yesterday? In that case, a penny may seem like the beginning of something big.

Jesus had great things to say about a widow who gave a gift of two pennies to her church. She wasn't the only one donating money at the church that day. There were lots of people—rich people—dropping off fat wads of cash. But Jesus told His disciples this woman had given the biggest gift of the day.

Those disciples must have thought Jesus wasn't very good at math. Then, Jesus explained that the other people had given a tiny

part of what they had. This woman had given everything, one hundred percent of what she owned. Others had given in *part*. She had given *all*.

You might feel that you don't have a lot to give. Especially right now. You're not a grown-up with a grown-up job and grown-up money.

You don't have a lot of money, but you do have love. But what do you do with it? Do you have to start a big charity to make a difference? And besides, if you just give a few pennies to your church or to a charity, can that really help someone?

They can, if you're the one who needs those few pennies. Did you know that just twenty-five pennies can provide a healthful meal for a school student in Kenya, Africa? (Source: World Food Programme.)

By the way, God loves it when you give those pennies because you *want to*, not because you feel like you should.

In the New Testament, the apostle Paul writes, "You must each decide in your heart how much to give. And don't give reluctantly or in response to pressure. 'For God loves the person who gives cheerfully'" (2 Corinthians 9:7 NLT).

God isn't impressed by how much money or stuff you have to give or donate. To Him, generosity is measured by the size of your heart.

It might be your pennies. It might be your time, talent, toys, or clothes. Whatever it is, God can use small gifts to do great things.

Whoever has the gift of giving to others should give freely.

ROMANS 12:8 NCV

May God be gracious to you and bless you
and make His face shine upon you.
May the good things you do be known,
So that people may praise the God
who made you and loves you.

INSPIRED BY PSALM 67:1

A Friend in High Places
(Really, Really High Places)

If tonight's sky is clear, take a few moments to gaze up at the stars. Do you know that the light you are seeing is actually thousands of years old? In fact, some stars are so old that, by the time their light reaches us, they have already burned out. Gone kaput!

You might know that our sun is a star. It's a big star, but did you know that there are many, many stars that are much bigger than our sun? One star in the Eta Carinae star system outshines the sun the same way a huge forest fire outshines one small birthday candle.

Let's talk about another kind of star—the neutron star. If you could take a soup spoon and scoop just one spoonful of one neutron star, that one little spoonful would weigh as much as three thousand humongous aircraft carriers!

Our God sure created an amazing universe, didn't He? God is powerful enough to create a big and spectacular world, and He is powerful enough to raise His son Jesus from the dead. But did you know that this power is available to *you*? The Bible puts it this way: "If the alive-and-present God who raised Jesus from the dead moves into your life, he'll do the same thing in you that he did in Jesus, bringing you alive to himself" (Romans 8:11 MSG).

Whenever you gaze up at the sun or the nighttime stars, remember that God is your friend in high places. The same God who built the universe wants to help you build a great life.

I am the one who made the earth and created
people to live on it. With my hands I stretched out
the heavens. All the stars are at my command.

ISAIAH 45:12 NLT

God says,
"Though the mountains be shaken
and the hills be removed,
my unfailing love for _____
will not be shaken.
Nor will my covenant of peace for
_____ be removed.
For I am the LORD, who has compassion
on _____.

INSPIRED BY ISAIAH 54:10

God's Restart Button

Do you like to play video games? A lot of kids do, but you have to be careful with them. They can gobble up your time like a hungry lion.

Have you ever goofed up really early in a video game and decided to hit RESTART? Maybe you told yourself, "That first try was just for practice."

In real life, of course, we don't always get a do-over. If you say something mean to a friend, you can't put those words back in your mouth and pretend they were never heard. If you are playing soccer and you miss the goal, you can't make everyone stop the match so that you can shoot again.

Fortunately, God *does* give us some do-overs. And no matter what we've done or what we have said, He still loves us, and He will always forgive us. If we say we are sorry when we do something wrong, God will hit the restart button for us. And He won't hold our sins against us. Isn't it great to have a loving God who can give us a fresh start?

Happy is the person
whose sins are forgiven,
whose wrongs are pardoned.

PSALM 32:1 NCV

All praise to the God
who has been our merciful
shepherd throughout life.
May the God of me and my ancestors,
the God who has rescued us from much harm,
bless this little one.
May wonderful _____ be blessed,
like my fathers and their fathers before them.

INSPIRED BY GENESIS 48:15–16

Risking Your Life for Bird Spit?

What would you be willing to risk for a little bit of bird spit?

Maybe you should hear a little story, a true story, before you answer.

Thailand's Phi Phi Islands are home to some unusual treasure hunters. The Phi Phis have lots and lots of limestone cliffs, some of them higher than a super-high-rise building! The treasure hunters risk their lives climbing these cliffs, in search of something they call White Gold. The White Gold is the spit of a bird called a swift. Have you ever done a craft project using white glue? Swift spit looks and feels kind of like that glue. Gross, huh?

The swifts use their spit to hold their nests together, and the treasure hunters gather as many nests as they can, so they can sell them. Many of their customers are restaurants who make soup out of the swifts' nests. If someone offered you a bowl of "Bird's Nest Soup," would you try some? You would need a lot of money. One bowl of this soup costs sixty bucks—and sometimes even more!

Why so expensive? Some people believe that swift spit is a kind of miracle medicine. They think it can help old people feel young and strong again. And they believe that it can cure breathing problems and fight off various diseases. This is why the treasure hunters can sell their nests for thousands and thousands of dollars! For them, bird spit is a precious treasure.

This brings us to a question: What do YOU treasure? It might be your video games. It might be your best friend or parents or grandparents. Caring deeply about something or someone can be a very good thing. But it is important to care about the *right* things, and it is so important to keep God at the top of that list. You see, God is the one who helps us love others, and He is the one who can help us avoid putting too much importance on something silly— like, perhaps, bird spit!

So be a treasure hunter every day, but seek God and the riches He wants you to have. God promises that everyone who looks for Him will find Him. No treasure map or cliff-climbing necessary! And no spit either.

Where your treasure is, there your heart will be also.

MATTHEW 6:21 NKJV

May the treasure of God's blessed
love be always with you,
the love that shines from the outside upon you,
like the warming sun,
and the love that glows inside
of your precious heart,
like a candle with an everlasting flame.

What's in a Name?

Do you know the reason behind your first name? Does it have special meaning? For example, the name Belle means beautiful.

Alexander means defender.

Bonnie means pretty.

Harvey means battle-worthy.

Galen means calm.

Diana means heavenly.

Cara means beloved.

Jason means healer.

Hunter means...well, *hunter*!

Perhaps you are named after someone. Do you know why you are named after this person?

Most moms and dads put a lot of thought into naming their children. It is an important job. Parents want their children to live up to their names. One couple named their daughter Olivia, because they wanted her to grow up to be kind and sweet, like another Olivia they knew.

Did you know that the name "Christian" hasn't been around forever? It didn't pop up until after Jesus Christ's death and resurrection. But soon after this miraculous event, Jesus' followers started to be called "Christians," which means "followers of Christ."

"Christian" is another name we should try to live up to. It is such an honor to be known as a follower of Jesus Christ, and we should work hard to be like Jesus, in what we do and what we say.

A good name is to be chosen rather than great riches, loving favor rather than silver and gold.

PROVERBS 22:1 NKJV

Grace and peace to you
from God our Father
and the Lord Jesus Christ.

1 CORINTHIANS 1:3 NCV

Your Solid Rock

There once was a huge rock that rested on the shore of a mighty sea. Many times, the sea's huge waves would splash over and against the rock, but the rock held firm. It didn't budge an inch.

During summer, the hot sun beat down on the rock. Some of the wildflowers near the rock wilted and died, but the sun didn't seem to bother the rock one bit.

Fall brought downpours of rain. The rain and wind washed away dirt, leaves, and bits of litter near the rock. But the rock itself didn't move.

In wintertime, the sea froze solid. Its waters turned to ice, hard like stone. But the rock stayed...well, a rock.

A brother and sister named Dwayne and Desiree loved to play on the rock. They climbed it and jumped on top of it. Sometimes they gathered their friends and all of them pushed against the rock as hard as they could. The rock didn't even wiggle.

When storms came, Dwayne and Desiree liked to hide near the rock. It helped protect them from the winds and rains.

Over the years, Dwayne and Desiree changed. Instead of jumping and playing on the rock, they liked to sit on the rock and talk about life. One day, they talked about how God is like their huge rock. He is big and powerful. Nothing can push Him around or change Him. You can depend on Him, because He will always be there for you!

I love you, LORD.
You are my strength.
The LORD is my rock, my protection,
my Savior. My God is my rock.
I can run to him for safety.
He is my shield and my saving strength, my defender.

PSALM 18:1–2 NCV

Dear God, our rock,

Please keep this wonderful child from all harm.

Watch over this precious life.

Going out and returning home.

Guard _____, both

now and forevermore.

INSPIRED BY PSALM 121:7–8

Who Needs Enemies?

Of all the Bible's commandments, this might be the toughest one to obey: "Love your enemies."

Think about those words. We are supposed to do more than pretend to like our enemies. More than just put up with them—even though they are so, so annoying. Jesus said to love them. Even if they are mean. Like some kid who picks on you or makes fun of you. Or a grumpy neighbor who doesn't seem to like kids like you.

Loving an enemy is really hard to do. That's why prayer is so important. Pray that you'll have the patience to show love—and pray that your enemy will see that you are trying to be nice.

You might also need to pray about your own feelings toward an enemy. That way, even if your prayers don't change an enemy's bad behavior or bad attitude, they will still change you.

As you pray for your enemies and try to be nice to them, remember that God loves them, just as He loves you. And He loves you even when you don't behave the way you should.

Finally, remember that if you show kindness to someone who is causing you trouble, you can reduce your list of enemies by one— and you might even add someone to your list of friends. It could happen—really!

I tell you, love your enemies. Help and give without expecting a return. You'll never—I promise—regret it.

LUKE 6:35 MSG

Heavenly Father,
May You clothe this child with compassion,
kindness, humility, meekness, and patience.
Help _____ to be patient
with troublemakers, to forgive, and
ask for forgiveness too.
Above all, wrap this wonderful kid in
love, which can bring us all together.
And let the peace of Christ be ruler
of this small and precious heart.

INSPIRED BY COLOSSIANS 3:12–15

A Picture of Peace

Years ago, a woman created a watercolor painting. It showed her husband leaning into heavy winds and driving rains during a spring thunderstorm. In one arm, the man cuddled his baby daughter, using his big overcoat to shield her from the storm. Despite the storm, the baby was sleeping soundly. The woman titled her painting "Peace." Do you think that's a good title for a painting with a storm in it? Why do you think that mom picked that title?

In life, true peace—peace of the heart—isn't about dodging all problems or trouble. Peace is all about trusting a loving heavenly Father, who is with us always. And He is especially close to us when life's storms rage all around us.

Here are a few ways to help you experience God's peace, especially when you are scared, sick, worried, or mad.

Focus on our all-powerful God, not on the thing that is bothering you.

Pray to God and ask that His peace will calm your heart.

Find someone to talk with you, hug you, and love you. (Moms and dads are great at this. So are grandmas and grandpas, big brothers and sisters, and best friends.)

Ask someone to help you learn a poem, song, or Bible verse that you can read, sing, or say when you need an extra dose of God's peace. (You might even choose one of the Bible verses, prayers, or blessings in this book. That would make the author really happy.)

Remember, God has promised to be with you always. And wherever God is, His peace is there too!

Where God's love is, there is no fear, because God's perfect love drives out fear.

1 John 4:18 NCV

Deep peace of the running waves to you,
Deep peace of the flowing air to you,
Deep peace of the quiet earth to you,
Deep peace of the shining stars to you.
Deep peace of the shades of night to you,
Moon and stars always giving light to you,
Deep peace of Christ, the Son of Peace, to you.

TRADITIONAL GAELIC BLESSING

"I Don't Wanna Bug God!"

Do you ever feel a little guilty asking God for something? After all, He has lots of big problems to deal with: wars, famine, pollution, crime, disease, and much, much more.

But give God a chance. He might surprise you with how much He cares, even about the so-called little things.

Jesus cared enough about lots of rumbling, grumbling stomachs that—more than once—He provided food for people who came to hear Him teach. He even cared enough about His disciple Peter's tax problem to provide him a coin to pay his taxes. He cared that people

at a wedding would run out of drinks so He miraculously provided
so that all of the wedding guests would have something to drink.

So don't hesitate to pray about anything. Whether your problems
are big or small, Jesus wants them all!

Are any of you in trouble? Then you should pray.

JAMES 5:13 NIrV

Oh, God, our Father,
Stay always with _____.
In the morning,
In the evening,
by day or by night,
always be there.

INSPIRED BY A TRADITIONAL POLISH BLESSING

Go, Lemmings, Go!

Lemmings are small rodents who migrate in huge, furry masses.
Sometimes this practice leads to disaster, as one lemming might
blindly follow another as he tumbles off a high cliff or ledge.

This is one reason there are no sports teams called the
Lemmings. After all, who would want to be named after a critter that
carelessly follows its buddies, even to its own doom?

However, a kid today can become like a lemming if he or she tries too hard to impress friends or do whatever other kids are doing—even if it is wrong or dangerous.

Let's face it: We all want to be popular, and we want the people around us to think we are cool. This is why Jesus is such a great example for us. He just didn't care about being cool. He hung out with unpopular people. He helped sick people—people so sick that most others didn't even want to get near them.

We should always remember that our goal is to be faithful to Jesus, not be popular or cool. Choosing friends wisely is a great way to stay on track. Singer TobyMac says it this way: "You are who you roll with." That means that kids should find friends who help each other grow closer to God, not lead each other into trouble.

Sometimes, people might make fun of Christians for living the right way. People sure made fun of Jesus, after all. But whatever people might call you, you can tell them, "Hey, at least I am not a *lemming!*"

And do not be conformed to this world, but be transformed by the renewing of your mind, that you may prove what is that good and acceptable and perfect will of God.

ROMANS 12:2 NKJV

A BLESSING OF ST. IGNATIUS

Lord Jesus, teach us to be generous;

teach us to serve You as You deserve,

to give and not to count the cost,

to fight and not to heed the wounds,

to toil and not to seek for rest,

to labor and not to seek reward,

except that of knowing that we do Your will.

Note to grown-ups: This prayer was adapted from St. Ignatius of Loyola, a sixteenth-century Spanish knight who dedicated his life to Jesus after being seriously wounded in battle. St. Ignatius was a fierce man of prayer, just as he was a fierce knight. He often spent seven hours a day communing with his Lord Jesus.

God's Calling—It's for You!

The God of the entire universe longs to spend time with *you*! Let that truth sink in for a moment. It's amazing, but true.

Many of us would consider it the chance of a lifetime to—just once—talk with our favorite singer, athlete, or TV or movie star. We would be eager to tell our friends all about it.

Unfortunately, we don't always show the same excitement for communicating with God, who loves us and who is far more fascinating than any big-shot we could ever meet.

God created the universe and everything in it—including the famous people we admire. He created us to have a relationship with Him. And the only way to have a relationship with *anyone* is to spend time with him or her. With God, this time can include prayer, meditation, reading the Bible or Christian books, listening to music, and worship.

The Lord of all creation wants to be close to you. You might not know Him super well yet, but He knows you. He wants to hear from you. He wants to talk with you—right now and always!

Don't worry about anything; instead, pray about everything. Tell God what you need, and thank him for all he has done.

PHILIPPIANS 4:6 NLT

My little heart is Yours to keep.
Warm it gently while I sleep.
My little soul to You belongs.
For every day of my life long.
Love me, Jesus, good and mild,
Keep me always Your dear child.

The Mystery of the Spirit Wind

Late one afternoon, a warm gust of wind stirred the ashes of a dying campfire—causing a glowing ember to pop into flame.

Then the wind moved on, swishing through leaves on the trees and swaying the branches this way and that. A flying squirrel used the wind to glide from one tree to another.

Next, the wind traveled toward the sea. It whipped up high waves and rocked boats like cradles.

Near the seashore, a young boy felt the wind at his back, so he stooped down and plucked a dandelion from the ground. He blew gently on the dandelion's fluffy white top, and its seeds took off on the wind, drifting and spinning like tiny parachutes.

Nearby, a girl and her babysitter launched a kite into the wind. The kite rose, soared, and dipped—like a crazy bird.

When the boy and the girl and the babysitter gazed out at the sea, they could see a sailboat being pushed along as the wind filled its giant sails.

Later on, the boy and girl talked about the amazing wind. They couldn't see the wind, but they could see how it moved the boats and the kite and the seeds. And they could smell the scents the wind brought with it—the damp-but-sweet smell of the sea. And they could feel its warmth on their faces and the gentle way it ruffled their hair.

As the boy and girl walked toward their homes, the babysitter told them, "You know, God's Spirit is kind of like the wind. You can't see that Spirit, but it sure does a lot of work, without being seen. And we can see the results of that work all over the world—and in each of your little hearts."

The wind blows where it pleases....So it is
with everyone born of the Spirit.

JOHN 3:8

Dear Jesus, thank You for the
blessing of Your Spirit.
Let the wind of Your Spirit be
this little one's guide.
Let it be a warm wind of comfort
and also a cool wind of refreshment.
Let it bring peace and love.
Let it give life, today, tomorrow, and forever.

Say Good-bye to Guilt!

Do you sometimes feel bad—really bad—about some wrong thing you have done? Do you wonder if God could really forgive you for... *that*?

Take heart. Whatever your "that" is, you are in good company. Good, *forgiven* company. It's time to peel off those bad feelings and run into Jesus' loving, forgiving arms. It's simple. Just say you're sorry, and let Jesus' mercy and love take care of the rest.

Your sins, whatever they may be, are not bigger than Jesus' love and forgiveness. No matter what you have done, said, or thought in your head.

When Jesus died on the cross, He absorbed every wrong thing you have ever done—and ever will do. Kind of like a sponge absorbs dirty water or other messy stuff. The sin is no longer yours. Jesus made it His. The Bible says that Jesus "became sin." Then He died, taking all that sin down with Him. He was buried in a tomb, but He beat death and rose to life. The sin, however, stayed buried. You are free from it.

Here's another way to look at this forgiveness thing: Jesus became dirty to make you clean. He is pure enough, strong enough, tough enough, and loving enough to take on all the world's sins. That means yours too. That's the kind of friend Jesus is to you. He can live anywhere and everywhere in the universe, and He wants to live in your heart!

Always remember, nothing you've done—or ever will do— is bigger than Jesus' love and forgiveness.

Love covers over a multitude of sins.

1 PETER 4:8

Now to him who is able to do immeasurably
more than all we ask or imagine,
according to his power that is at work within us,
to him be glory...in Christ Jesus
throughout all generations,
forever and ever!
Amen.

EPHESIANS 3:20–21

Inside Every "Don't" Is a "Do"

Why did God give us so many rules to follow? Why is the Bible so full of all that "Thou shalt not" stuff? Did God create people just so He would have someone to boss around?

Look at it this way: When you were really little, why were you told NO! every time you tried to touch a hot stove or a sharp knife?

Why doesn't a teacher let her students play in the busy street during recess? Why does a doctor tell her patient to quit smoking before she gets really sick—or worse?

A toddler *wants* to touch the stove because it *looks like* touching something orange and glowing might be fun. And those students might want to play in the street because being stuck in the schoolyard is boring.

At the moment a kid sees a bunch of rules, his first thought might just be, "I don't like these rules; I wonder if I can break some of them without getting in trouble."

Unfortunately, sometimes we don't think about how rules are meant to protect us and make us safe and happy.

Obeying God's commandments gives us protection, peace of mind, and good health—healthy spirits as well as healthy bodies and minds. That's why the God who loves us and wants to see us succeed has given us rules to live by.

And it's important to understand that all the Bible's "don'ts" are really just another way of saying "do."

For example, the commandment that tells us, "Don't wish you had other people's stuff" is another way of saying DO appreciate *your* stuff. Be grateful for it. Get true joy from your stuff by not comparing it with someone else's.

The commandment "Don't steal" has a "DO" inside too: DO respect others' things. Just as you would want them to respect your things. If you want more things, go out and earn them. That will make you feel a lot better than stealing them.

If you have been viewing the Ten Commandments or other Bible rules as a big stick God uses to whack people, it's time to think differently. God is for you, not against you. And so are His rules.

How blessed you are to have a Lord and Savior who cares enough to provide rules to help you enjoy the best life possible!

Your word is a lamp to my feet and a light for my path.

PSALM 119:105

Blessed is this child who has obeyed
God even when it's hard to do.
May _____ receive the
rewards You have promised
to those who love You and obey You.

INSPIRED BY JAMES 1:12

The Car Wreck
That Changed a Kid's Life

On a lonely Illinois road, a sixteen-year-old kid named Thomas Weller struggled to drive home in a blizzard. But the slick roads and strong winds were too much for him. He lost control of his car and smashed into a snowbank, leaving him helplessly stuck on a stormy and freezing night.

Shaken but unhurt, Thomas sat in his car and waited. And waited. Unfortunately, he seemed to be the only person around. For the longest time, there wasn't another car or truck in sight.

Finally, someone stopped—a man who helped Thomas free his car from the snowbank. Before long, the grateful teenager was home, safe and warm. Later that night, Thomas realized something: *There wasn't any other traffic out there tonight. That man probably saved my life!*

The act of mercy changed Thomas's life. Today, that young boy is in his sixties, and he is known as "The San Diego Highwayman." He drives a classic old car around nearby roads, on the lookout for drivers who are stuck or stranded. He's been on this mission of mercy for almost fifty years, ever since he crashed his car into that Illinois snowbank. An auto mechanic by trade, Thomas has helped more than six thousand drivers, filling up empty gas tanks, changing flat tires, and pouring coolant into hissing radiators. He's helped scared and lonely teenagers, church youth-group vans, and buses full of soccer and volleyball players.

Thomas accepts no pay for his services. He asks only that the people he helps pass the mercy along the next time they meet someone in trouble.

Long ago, Jesus preached a sermon to a crowd on a mountainside. He said, "Blessed are the merciful, for they will be shown mercy." Thomas Weller is a living example of Jesus' words. Some of the people Thomas helps cry because they are so grateful. Others try to pay him for his help. But Thomas is motivated by Jesus, not money. He just wants to share the gift of mercy—one of the most beautiful gifts of all. And mercy is a gift anyone can give. You don't have to be a grown-up or have lots of money. You can give mercy, and mercy is a gift that has a way of spreading to lots of people. It is a gift that keeps on giving.

Blessed are the merciful, for they will be shown mercy.

MATTHEW 5:7

God of mercy and compassion,
We know how good it feels when
someone shows us kindness,
especially when that kindness is
undeserved or unexpected.

Help us to avoid hogging those good, warm feelings.
Please inspire us to show mercy
every time we get the chance.
Help us to remember that one good deed
can make someone's whole day,
and maybe even change a life.

The Day EVERYONE Flunked Sunday School

Have you ever had to take a test in Sunday school? What do you think of that idea? Shouldn't tests be only for regular school?

Recently, a teacher of a Sunday school full of kids like you prepared a test for all his boys and girls. The test had just one question. Here it is:

List the five best Sunday school lessons I have ever taught you.

How do you think the kids did on this test? (How would *you* do?)

If you guessed, "They flunked!" you are exactly right! A few kids remembered a lesson or two—usually the most recent ones. A few wrote answers like, "I really liked that one lesson about Jesus. And God."

When some of them complained that the test was too hard, the teacher tried to make things easier. "Okay," he said, "you don't have to list the five *best* lessons. Just list ANY five Sunday school lessons that you can remember."

Do you think that helped?

Nope. Everyone still flunked.

Then the teacher collected all of the test papers and tore them up. He handed everyone a brand-new sheet of paper.

"Let's try something different," he said. "This time, please list the five people who are most important to you. The ones who love you most and help you the most in your life."

How do you think the kids did this time?

Yep, everyone got an A-plus-plus! It was pretty easy to make a list of important, helpful, and loving people. Some kids listed way more than five names. Some had ten. Others listed twenty or more. Moms and dads made the list. Foster parents. Grandmas and grandpas. Teachers, coaches, and babysitters. Even some sisters and brothers. Quite a few dogs and cats made the list too. Also, one gerbil.

This Sunday school teacher didn't give that first test to make the kids feel bad. He just wanted to teach them something. (And it's NOT that his Sunday school lessons weren't very good!) He wanted to help them understand that *people* are important. People are like "living Sunday school lessons," because they show us how the Bible is put into action!

It is people who make a difference in others' lives. Remember always to be thankful for the good people God has placed in your life. And try really hard to be the kind of person who makes others' lives better and happier.

> *As God's chosen people, holy and dearly loved,*
> *clothe yourself with compassion, kindness,*
> *humility, gentleness, and patience.*
>
> COLOSSIANS 3:12

God of love and kindness,

May this beloved child do all kinds of good things,

In all kinds of wonderful ways,

In places near and far,

In the morning, at noon, and at night,

To all kinds of people,

Today, tomorrow, and forever.

INSPIRED BY A CHARLES WESLEY POEM

Acknowledgments

The themes for the devotions "Your Solid Rock" (page 117) and "The Mystery of the Spirit Wind" (page 133) were inspired by an imaginative children's book titled *God Is Like...*, by Julie Walters. This book, now apparently out of print, was published by WaterBrook in 2000.

Special thanks to all of the children—in churches, schools, libraries, homes, bookstores, coffee shops, and auditoriums across the country—who allowed me to share many of these stories and concepts with them.